MW00679486

SEASON OF DREAMS

Two Weeks Alone
in the Peaked Hill Dunes

Jonathan A. Wright

Brook Hollow Press
Hatfield, Massachusetts

First edition

Table of Contents

Dedication

To all those sailors, wanderers, dreamers, beach walkers, painters, swimmers, playwrights, writers, fisherman, poets, sun worshipers and all who have come to the dune shacks before me, especially those who have inhabited and given life to the three prior now-washed-out-to-sea incarnations of the Margot Gelb shack, and also to those who have yet to come, who will know the place in a new way all their own, thank you.

Preface

For two weeks in the late spring of 2017, I was drawn toward the farther edge of the familiar. All the explosive subtleties of the Outer Cape — its sand and weather and color and wind — were at hand; at times ferocious and at times muted. I was a willing captive.

Too much can be made of the idea of precipices and pivotal moments, but the dunes offered me the largest possible aperture through which to look at, and to approach up close, the points of contact, friction and gentleness between myself, my inner world, and the physical place. All the supple geologic suddenness of a seemingly uneventful landscape was laid bare to startle me awake.

The Peaked Hill Dunes, and their offshore ancient remnants, the Peaked Hill Bars, make up the back of the wrist and the outstretched forearm of the Outer Cape. Facing north from here in late spring, the sun rises from and sets into the ocean. Walking in either direction on the beach, the arm of the Cape slowly curves away, so that neither where I have come from nor where I am going is visible beyond a knuckle or two of sand and bluffs. The only expanse is the sea, which rolls away to its horizon. The only barriers are the ocean's chill, and myself.

This book does not so much chronicle dreams as track the daily evidence of their presence. Simply put, the dreams are not new, but the season of their liveliness is renewed. Within that fluid decompression lies an edge of mortality, more tidal than surf. The dreams are those we have overnight during sleep, while at rest, while walking, waiting, and while writing. The ones we have for our lives on earth.

Many apparent obstacles are temporal, or time driven. "Time sensitive" is the onshore phrase. This is more of a social compact than fact. During this shack time, I read about the hunting practices of the native people of northern British Columbia, in Hugh Brody's magnificent book <u>Maps and Dreams</u>. In this narrative, the native people await an inner call from the animal, and only then act on the hunt. What struck me over and over was the apparently chaotic and wandering nature of the preparation, which in fact tracked a deeper process of awaiting the dream of the animal and the summons. So, too, it is with writing in a single place for a time. I can listen, record, and wait. I must wait. The incoming tide may find the sea buckling with fresh weed or clear as glass. It keeps its own counsel.

Another gift, also from my friend and mentor Robin Barber, came along for this time. A fresh reading of Jane Benyus's <u>Biomimicry</u> provides insight into the science and mystery of natural regeneration. How perfect here, where my own writing and inner life were being restored in the normal course of time in the shack, so much that might interfere, left back at the intersection of Snail Road and Route 6.

Just a few centuries ago, these Outer Cape lands were fully forested, until Europeans arrived and cut down all the trees for boatbuilding, cooperage, shelter and fuel. The settlers created, in the aftermath, a kind of desert. The soil washed away or was blown into the bay. What we live in now is the still-early healing of those wounds, with constant setbacks. I look at them up close in the *In the Hollows* folio and poems. The earth will heal herself if we will just let her be!

Writing in the dunes shack is like walking the beaches and the dune trails: hard climbs, great views, slow slides, exquisite glades, magical water. I am no stranger to pressing for, and being pressed by, promised outcomes. No business career is complete without those many tyrannies. But, as it happened, the daily beginning and onward scrolling of text, classified only as *Day Seven* or *Day Ten*, provided the core materials, and in some cases the actual lines, for what is written here. The transformation process of gathering, discovering and shaping the meaning of the work has taken many months.

Although I am new to these dunes, I am a creature of place. We are all creatures of place to some degree. This book was seeded, raised, nourished and harvested from the dunes. It required some additional preparation and further simmer back onshore. The work seemed at first to be artifact of the place and time, tied to the narrative of living in the shack. Gradually it has shifted, inhaled and discovered its own momentum.

Probably the sweetest revelation of this time comes through the camera lens. I am visually oriented, and have made many promises to myself about photographic activities. Here, by self-assignment, are walks with camera in hand, with no constraints other than keeping the camera dry, avoiding nesting habitat, and being back to the shack by dark. With hours to burn, the eye closes in on what it sees.

The camera brings the visual world inside the photographer's eye, body and heart. My eye gained a new focus and focal length through this new daily practice of watching and taking in.

Whether I return to the shacks or not, the place itself is secured within me, and I can go there visually anytime. The gift of a lifetime. In words and images, I hope you find something here for your own journey.

I.

At the Shack

Here

Out to sea, old shorelines
stormed away and cut
to ribbons of sand
by thousands of winters
have left their ridges of ruin —
the Peaked Hill Bars.

Surf crashes there,
but in-shore it's calm
at half-tide —
my shack its own
protected cove,
imagined estuary
at the edge of the dunes.

I have taken quarters
in the clear curl of a wave,
in the surf and on the earth.

It's quiet here inside,
surrounded by green light
and the startle of ocean cold.

Salt spray tumbles the words —
a gravel wash.

Shack

The pump handle stiffens,
loads up with the first gush
of fresh and glistening well-water
sixty feet back from the bluff.

Driven rain soaks through
the clapboard privy roof.
The moist sweet smell
of evergreen forest
and old cedar chest.

The roof is tight, no drip pans needed.
Simple enough maybe, but rain here
comes from all directions at once,
especially sideways, and up.

Deepening cold reminds me
that an ancient ice sheet pushed
all this sand and gravel here.
Glaciers do that, grinding, heaving,
crushing and melting their way
out to sea.

The clothesline is salvaged anchor rope,
not the hardware store braided stuff.
Could be useful if the wind picks up,
tying down the shack — but to what?

Not many clothes pins, two handfuls —
just enough for how much line there is.
I was looking everywhere for window screens —
they're under the desk, against the wall.

Under the bed
the wood floor varnish remains;
elsewhere it is worn bare
by sandy feet and brooming clean.
The sap wood wears down,
leaving the hard pine knots as knuckle mounds.
Like limestone temple steps.

Three ways to make coffee, two for tea.
Lobster steamer and a Dutch oven ready,
for when the wind does not relent.

Dark enough mid-morning to light two oil lamps,
their flames the color of Meyer lemons.
Trim the wicks, set them on the table,
one in each east window.
To mariners, to the wrecked and the worn,
the walkers, writers and painters,
your cold is welcome here,
your bare and your wet.
My pen is ready; the table set.

Wait

In the hour before
a blood-orange dawn
peels back the quilted rind
of gray sky,

the dark swallows up
the grass and roses whole,
leaves a bright skin of sand.

Cold, still, damp and rain —
a hollow of inner thigh on
the languid body of dune
curves toward me —
dark, sweet, quiet, smooth.

Boardwalk on Four Sides

(at the Margo Gelb shack)

The sea is calm today —
the beach below pristine,
once I gather up today's haul,
human trash washed up.

Plovers, terns and sanderlings
get their seasons underway.
Over the bars, the water
is a clear willow-green.

The shack leans back
into its hill, feet planted deep
into the steep,
life-saving mostly done.
I have come alone
on a new path of rescue.

The north deck is five feet wide —
enough to sit on
in a lawn chair
and allow a friend to pass.
To wait and watch,
to reach the steps at the corner,
and swing the screen door out.

On a clear day like today
I can squint and follow the planet's curve
up and over Nova Scotia to Labrador,
to the Belle Isle Strait
with its fading glacial ice.

This docile, quiet, kindly sea
tore sixty feet off the bluffs
last winter, used it to fill
harbor channels at will.

The east deck is three feet wide;
that side has been damp and blowing
for three days, fog rolling in
across the four other shacks
in the hollows east of me.

That's my imaginary village down there,
old Jeeps parked askew,
an empty chair on the hill.
Foot traffic to their privy and back
is all. Little solar lights
twinkling at night.

Two steps down and a path
through the beach-rose thicket
lead to my privy,
a handsome and dreamy
skiff-like cupboard
up on its transom;
that's the corner where the clothesline
reels off, gathers midday sun
when there is some.

South is the back of the house,
decking buried into the sand;
shelters the propane tanks
and rubbish barrels.
I like to linger here —
it's the garage, what passes for
an engine room in the dunes
with no engine —
a place to hide when the winds rise.

Thumb-sized bumble bees
lurch among the rose blossoms.

The west deck looks down
to the main beach path —
nobody much walking in May midweek
except morning dog runs
and French and Russian tourists yesterday;
the air so calm
I heard their voices
as if they were sitting here
on the steps.
Lumber and repair supplies tucked under,
piles of old lobster buoys and beach debris.
Useful later maybe.

Euphoria shack is three sand-rises
to the west.
Wood smoke drifted over last night —
I sniffed it, sipped it like wine.

The sunset lights up the vapor trails
of eastbound jets
night-coursed for Europe;
further north, vast steam pillows,
from the Seabrook nuclear plant I guess,
gather and send their plumes.

Here on the western deck,
the last of the sun and shadow
linger on.

Hiding me from sun and wind,
or embracing them,
the shack invites me
to settle, to slow, to stay.
To let the weather go and come;
to slowly come undone.

Whale Watching From Bed

Dreaming, I tugged and tugged
at your sleeve.
"Come, come!" I said,
"See the whales!
No, no, not through
the salt-crusted window glass —
come to the door, wide open!

"See the long fleets of them
in wild formation,
white flanks rising and falling,
just off the beach,
heading toward Truro!"

The morning sea is smooth,
wind-scrubbed down to calm;
sunlight gleams off
the long flat wake patches
where the whales must have
earlier passed.

Each of Us

With two lamps lit
in the shack windows,
I am in my wheelhouse,
of out-to-sea and long ago —
my home outside
of everything I know.

For you, the corner bed
up against the salty sidewall planks,
wreck-salvaged and reused,
quilts pulled up under your chin,
is home again.

Warm pools of light,
the spiders and damp of a childhood
snuggled at the edge of the big lake.
Stuffed animals and books piled high.
Wood smoke from the old library stove
drifts upstairs to you…

Here, my work table,
under one double window,
looks out across a seamless course
of North Atlantic.

My bed under the south double window
faces into the beach roses.

Shack life is wide open
unprotected shelter
hollowed out of time.

Rain dripping from the eaves —
no machines at work.
The fuel for light and warmth
is a quilt
of quiet and dreams.

Early Love

You poked out
of the swallow house early,
when birds wake up;

a bus driver's head out the window,
checking both ways.

Look at your fresh white smock,
slender legs, tiny bare feet,
feather-ruffed collar
and a shimmering
sea-glass-blue cape,
clasped around your throat!

Then you stand on the clothes line
and I want so much to call you
my indigo bunting.

Don't you remember?
Buntings are for parades and grand occasions!
You'll have your own motorcade;
you've been practicing
your solo since dawn,
waiting your turn on the county road.

Here come the antique Fords,
fire trucks with wooden ladders,
bands of horns and pipers.
Everyone is in costume.

How you look, the way you stand,
how little you say,
and this longing at midday,
reminds me of girls
with supple, two-syllable names,
whose green eyes,
or blue or brown,
bare necks
and how they turn slightly away
staring at something
over my left shoulder,
not quite in view,
got me started
loving birds.

Fling

One waits perched
on the bird-house post;
the other, in its navy-blue evening jacket,
comes calling.
Flutter and flight —
again and again, alight!

The conjugal moment is over
before I can light the candles
or summon the choir
of gulls.

Done with him, she ducks
back inside the house.
He was nothing special anyway.

The dinner-jacket guest
has taken up another post.
He checks the weather,
trolls for insects.
He gets his disheveled
feathers back in order,
lifts them into the wind
to be dry cleaned.

Water Love

Swimming is proof the sea
never tires of me;
minerals, water, salt,
and family;
the same love
as my human kin.

Kisses that linger on
the heart-shaped rock
left for me;
a finger on the lips
for a secret kept.

The tingling in the back of my hand
when I touch your face,
more when sleeping than awake.

Love accumulates its second natures
in second chances,
in ponds and hands,
in my body, on my wrists.

Promises surface slowly,
rise up, for keeping.

II.

Riddles of Sand

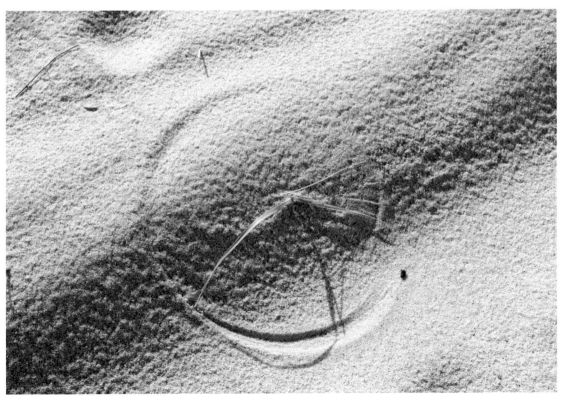

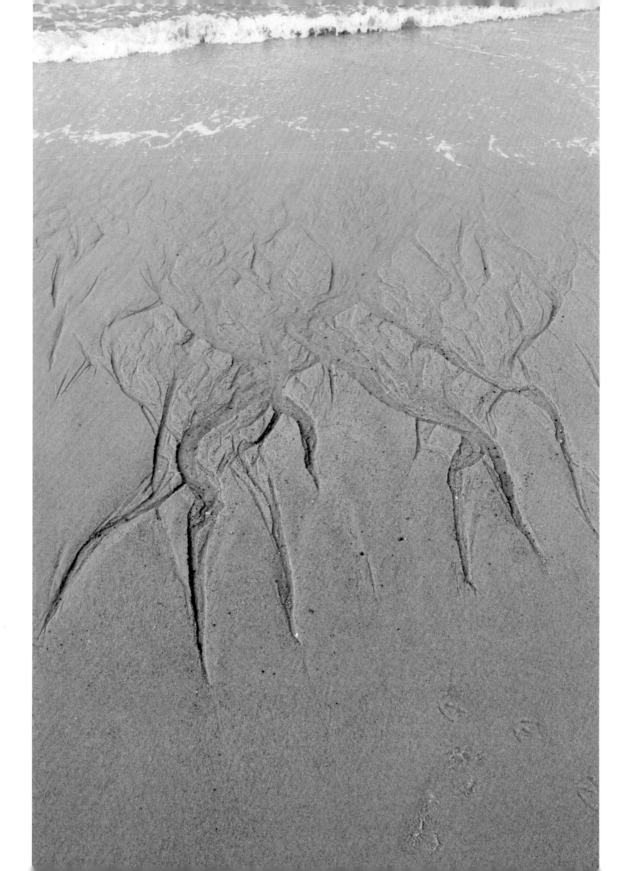

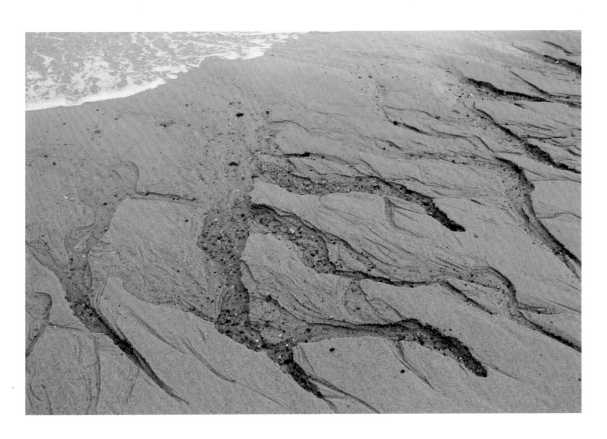

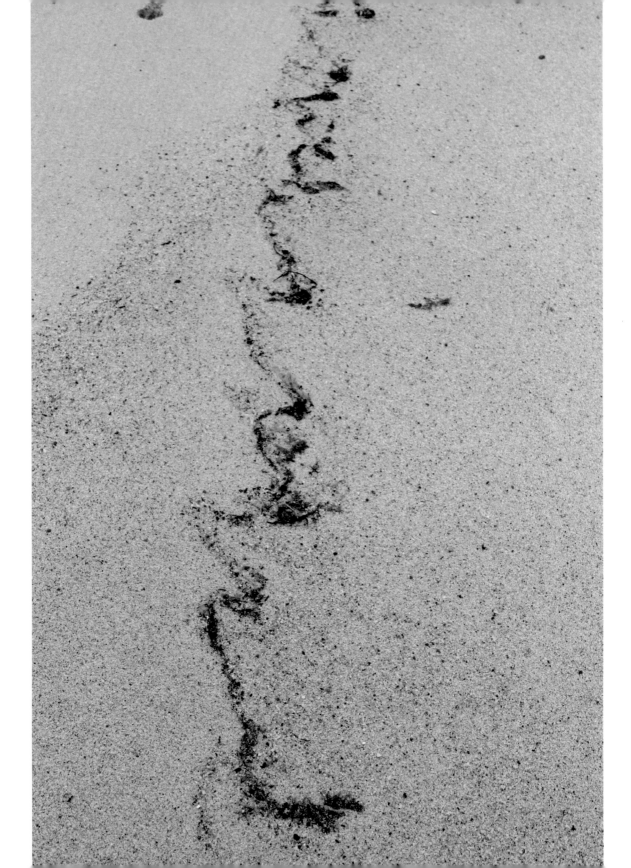

Outside

The Bars are shallowing
at the end of the ebb tide.
Four hundred years
of a thousand wrecked ships —
bones, wares and sailors
buried there.
Coast Guardsmen walked the shore at night
listening, watching, in the swing
of dim lamplight.

Cold water stories beckon.
Freezing seamen cry out at night.
Shredded rigging screams in a winter gale.
Sails in tatters, hatches torn away,
solitude, sand and dunes remain.

No signs of wreck or salvage now.
No losses are fully reckoned.

Quiet comes and an old terror
goes deep and waits.
The sun and cold are working
through their differences.

The wind has clocked southeast,
toward the deep green ocean and Gulf Stream
where a nor'easter gets its water.

No warming trend for now —
laundry on the line does not dry.

I can see my breath while eating lunch
squatting on the lee side.

Whale Watch

To see whales from the shack
I stay put; I watch the whale watchers
leaning on boat rails
watching for whales.

When the whale-watch boats
come close inshore,
I watch the water
around the boats;
just a bit of spout here and there
as seen from a porch chair.

No photo ops, no drama —
just ordinary whale life.

Feed, mate, swim, migrate unseen.
Minutes later the water is smooth, clean.

Diesel haze lingers.
Sky serene.

Three Kinds of Rain

Long after midnight,
cold, foggy, windless, gray,
thunder comes, slow and distant first,
then crashes into the shack like cymbals.
Torrents pound the roof;
I crouch under the waterfall.

Lightning arrives in force,
wrap the shack in dazzle.

Night, shadow, shape, color, space
all lost to blaze.
No building, no shelter —
just a shudder, a quickened gaze.

Nor'easter rain comes in hard —
frayed ropes whip
the shack windows —
water pellets explode,
streak down the glass.
It gusts and whines and lasts.
And lasts.

This morning's rain
is a child's shy knock
at the bedroom door,
asking for a story,
like the one about
scampering sanderlings,
tiptoeing on the roof,
pretending to be rain.

Or was it the rain instead
I mistook for birds?

Between Rains

Shades of light and gray,
strands of cotton wick and piping,
threaded in the sea and sky
between the rains.

I went to watch them weaving
from the high tide edge,
finding there instead
weeds of every shade of brown and red —
all the ocean's greenery and debris.

The sky is so big when the rain relents,
its water spent;
the air is clear,
opens out forever;

every grain of sand and imagined planet
scrubbed and gleaming.

Short on Company

Shack roof rain
sounds like sweeping water
across concrete
with a coarse corn broom.

Washing done, the sun
tries to burn through,
but clouds today are as thick and tough
as old tires.

So much water came down,
the air smells sweet,
more of soil and farm
than beach grass and sand.
Dune dirt is fresh, eager, lively.

My favorite swallow swoops in close
to check on me.

Short on company
at the edge of a cliff
and water-crazed,
it's good to be
on a first-name basis
with stars and birds —
something close by
when my heart and lungs
start banging around
in their musty sea chest.

The rusty hasp rattles.
Come on out I say.
It's not latched.

Losing Track

I have practiced for a long time
getting stuff done.
Being efficient
means getting more stuff done.
Success means getting the right stuff done.
More stuff. More doing. More done.

Make lists, organize errands.
Focus on the big picture.
Note the details.
Pay attention to the items
in my grocery cart.
Whose letters
have gone unanswered?
What bills are due soon?
What plans do I have
for this afternoon?

The shack door screen
shivers once or twice —
a visitor perhaps.
Then nothing more.

Keeping track is a busy life.
Losing track is decks awash
in a small boat.

I can swim.

By Ten

From dawn 'till now
the day is more than half done.

Two poems carved as timber or meat,
and poorly dressed.
Dreams unkempt, still heaving
and the bed's unmade.
Dishes done poorly, done again.

One pump trip, with priming;
privy visit, three rain squalls.
Four fishing boats
and a scallop dragger.

Ducks and cormorants so water-quick
they look like seal heads from the deck.
I am still and restless,
waiting for a sign of an end in sight
from which to begin again.

A hundred birds are busy —
it's hard work, eating your body weight
in bugs by ten,
then three more times by dusk.

Daybreak

Low-power fishing skiffs
idling outside the Bars
means a good day ahead.
Fishermen know.

The air is cool, still and damp.
Northerly waves break
in long white ribbons.

The sky hovers, shifting,
glowers down out to sea —
a rain shower lingers there;
sandy-hued fog rolls down the Cape
from the southeast.

Bakery-sweet, heady beach roses
open up in a vase on my work table —
I trimmed them from the privy path.
They love the sun and shelter there —
and the shelter here
of working hands.

Shifting

Brace first.
Lean into the wind,
then lean away.
Turn in toward the path,
down through the tiny bog.

The pine green, the red of berries;
a shifting light of sky and soil
are the artists-in-residence here.
Wind brushes. Spring solvent.
A palette of broken clouds,
mending leaves.
Quiet water. Stillness comes
as my breathing slows.

Wind passes higher and higher up
in the tops of scrub oak,
out of earshot now.

Another conversation begins.
Arrangements are underway.
The hollow and I exchange
looks and then nod.
It promises sweetness, thorns,
clouds of insects, and I,
unfamiliar patience.

Glide

The ocean is a blank stare,
gray with white creases
here and there.
Face pressed flat,
on ice or glass —
an oily glare.

Gulls glide to windward in pairs,
just above the bluff.

Marsh hawks are lower down,
search the grass and ground.

Watch the wings.
Wait your turn.

III.

In the Hollows

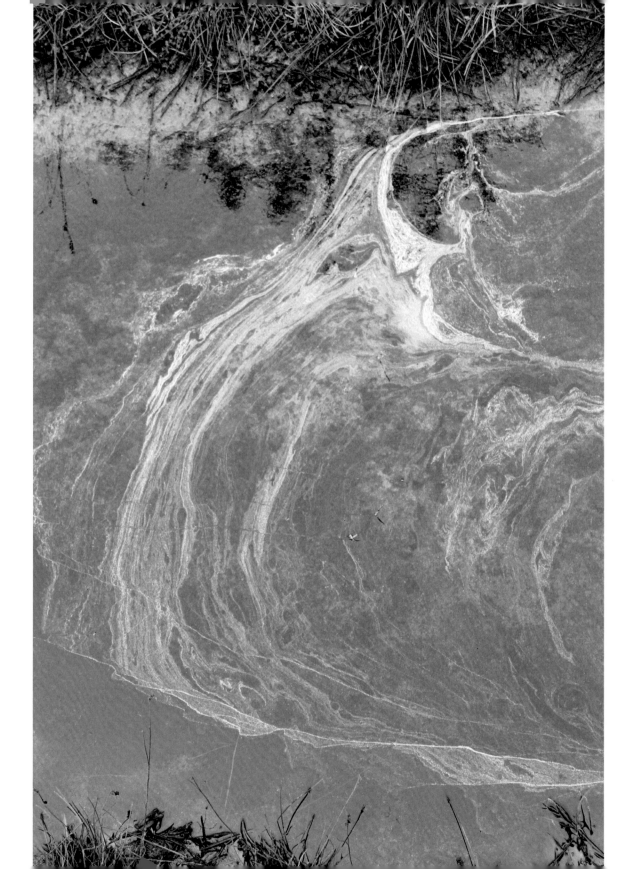

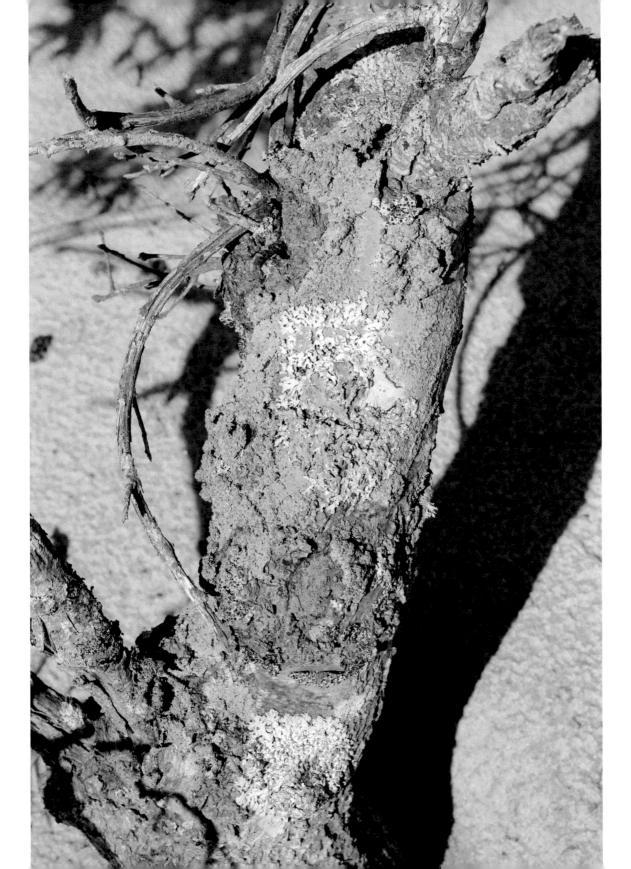

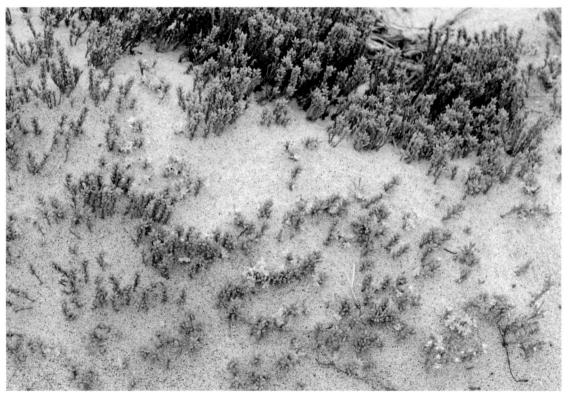

What's Coming

The door is wedged tight
with wood scraps and cardboard.
I can feel the wind
across the floor
from across the room.

Nor'easters will have their way with me.
They move everything sideways,
to the southwest.
Sand and gravel; shoals and birds,
bones, teeth, skin,
traces of tenderness.

This storm has me bundled,
my mind trussed up
in sailors' twine,
tumbling down the beach,
toward Race Point Light.

Memories of starlight,
beach fires and heat,
all the preparations and the thinking
have gone gray and dark.

Check the wash down there tomorrow
at low tide.
You'll know it's me
by the burn marks.
The scarring.

Hands and Body

Shingle gray everywhere:
clouds, shack and sea;
hazel-eye green of dune grass;
rugosa leaves and bayberry.
A charcoal sky
here and there — unfinished strokes
of drama, a smudge of mystery.

Unsettled weather settles
into my hollows —
the spaces cut away
and open.

See the puddle bottoms
holding water now —
shallow hands of rain.

Walk with Birds

Walking east toward Truro
at low tide,
the steep beach stretches down
the twelve-foot tidal drop;
smooth as skin,
sand curves, rolls and swells
like leg muscle.

Only gravel and sand here —
no rocks on the Outer Cape,
ten miles west
of the last moraine.

No tracks other than water birds.
I walk softly, carefully.
I have all day.
The terns are used to me,
scamper more slowly.

Sanderlings are waiting out
their spring, stopping over to rest;
next month Arctic-bound to nest.

On a flattened promontory
the sand gives way
to fissured gravel rivulets —
an aquifer running out
from underneath the land.
Sea birds love it here at low tide —
worms and crabs, tiny morsels,
brackish sand.

The beach is cordoned off with twine
above the high tide line —
a plover rookery of weeds and brush,
shells and beach debris.
The birds are only weed
and wood and stone until
their wings and muscles move.

Sand and grass
for thirty miles,
cove and point and bluff.
It's easy to be lost;
a journey on foot
around a chorus of curves.

I wait for the light to shift,
camera ready.
No one else has been here today;
no one else will come.

I feel lighter than usual,
begin to drift, unmoored.
As the shadows lengthen,
take on form,
something trembles
and stretches out ahead,
free of me.

Still Life

Green curl of a blue wave
washes to an ocean cream,
folds up and seeps away.

Look down
where the sand is steadied there.
See the miracle of every grain,
its browned and shadowed light
at the water line.

Look up. Dunes fold into sky.
The seams are sewn.
Clouds torn away.

Light in the Dark

White cloud-cover quilt
keeps the dune hollows sand-bright
and smooth overnight.
Grasses are still.

Fishing boats' deck lights
blaze to the north.
Men working all night.

Hollow

Black pines in the hollows
spread out as if on all fours,
picking out the pockets
of water and soil.
Scruffy bark and bristle tips
give way to purple and magenta succulents,
reaching for a summer
of seed and cone.

Soft yellow pollen
rain-washed
onto an apron band
on the sand below;
nearby it floats
in topographic patterns
on still black water
in abandoned Jeep tracks.

Tiny white mayflowers,
unfolding scrub-oak leaves
rimmed in red,
heather and lichen everywhere.
I thank them all. For kindness.
For community.
For their sunny and solitary dispositions.
For bravery.
For what the wind has
just for now
left alone.

Current

Tide is written
in estuary, rip and pool;
cold and respiration.

Four changes each day.
Slack is one long breath.

Never mind blue moons,
equinox surges and neap tides;
follow the swells
lifting underneath.

They raise and drop my pen
like a driftwood limb.

My weathered body,
with its strange loyalties and wildness
lashed alongside,
will do the rest.

Shack Drama

The way the weather changes
I could set my watch,
make dinner plans.

Rain comes in the way
lights go down at the theater —
it's a matinee!

Sun comes out
for a curtain call.

The evening show
is candlelit
for the better dressed.

An orchestra of stars.

Warming Trend

I propped the door open at last —
it's a new world out there, free of rain.
Cold has flattened its viscous thickness
out onto the sand,
slipped back over the bluff,
and out into the sea.

Light wind through the door screen,
surf and rose rustle;
bright blue bird swoop,
wing bustle and warm.

Wet locker lid thrown back,
oilskins hung out.
Cold releases its claim.

Seeing Out

The world is born again
inside each surprise.

Earth and human healing
in a burst of sunrise.

Air and breath together;
flame, fuel, feel.

Ocean and spring water magic
hide in plain sight.
Bank the fire. Spread the light.

Botany, temple and church;
uncertainty and mercy lurk
where day breaks.

Odysseys roll out
over the widening sand.

See how the mind
slips out from behind
a cardboard cutout of itself,
still unsteady, waving off the rain squalls
one by one,

how it stands, willowing,
bent double, in the open,
seeing everything
for the first time.

IV.

Edges of Day

Acknowledgements

This two-week residency in the Boris Margo and Jan Gelb shack came up quickly, sooner than I could have hoped, and in many ways just in time. I am immensely grateful to Outer Cape Artists Residency Collaborative (OCARC) for their careful review and support, and to all the volunteers who create and envision and enliven the shack community. Janet Whelan and the OCARC Board were receptive, kind, and encouraging. I am awed by the level of volunteer effort and depth of commitment evidenced by their work and the work of others. Thank you for continuing on! The long-term commitment of the Peaked Hill Trust is breathtaking.

Mariellen was my delivery caretaker, and David extricated me. Both were wonderful and hospitable in just the right ways. Mariellen made it clear she was the shack's caretaker, not mine, and if I needed anything it was probably already there. Such a great message, and so true, as the shack was quite complete, as if on board a boat offshore, thereby offering measures of both liberation and comfort. Need tweezers, a piece of rope, more matches, a poncho? It's all there.

None of this could or would have happened without the support and extraordinary encouragement of my friend and artist Russell Steven Powell. For his faith, friendship and fun I am so very grateful. Book designer Christopher Weeks brought incredible patience, talent, and superb creative and supple eye, to the making of this book. My wife Meg Kelsey Wright offers deep and unwavering encouragement, and an editor's keen eye, along with the timely care and wisdom as is her way in the world.

Poets Carol Edelstein and Pat Schneider crafted encouraging recommendations for my OCARC application. I am awed to count them as generous, wise and thoughtful friends.

My gratitude extends without boundary to all who read, listen, comment, encourage, correct, support, critique and otherwise advance another's writing. Without you we are but mumbles.

Author Notes

Jonathan A. Wright has written for many years. His first book of poetry, *After the Rain*, was published in 2014 by Gallery of Readers Press. Two chapbooks, *November Suite* and *Bending Outward*, were completed in 2012 and 2016 respectively. His work is included in two recent releases of the *Gallery of Readers Anthology*. He is a regular guest columnist in local media.

He has been an owner of Wright Builders Inc., in Northampton, MA., since its founding in 1974. The firm is a New England leader in sustainable design and construction, having completed two Living Buildings in 2016, and more than 50 LEED certifications. He writes and teaches on sustainability as well.

He is a 1974 graduate of Hampshire College in Amherst, MA, where he was a member of the first entering class, and studied with Michael Benedikt, David Smith, Francis Smith and others. He is an avid sculler, and maintains US Rowing coaching certification.

He thrives on collaborations with other artists, including ongoing projects with painter Russell Steven Powell. He lives with his wife, pianist Meg Kelsey Wright, in Northampton, Massachusetts.